How to Use This Guide

In this guide we suggest a variety of strategies for becoming not just a better student but a master student. Some are simple. Others require further explanation and clarification. For example, if you are motivated to improve, you can immediately implement Idea #15 (from **"18 Ideas for Becoming a Master Student"**): "Test yourself before you come to class by trying to summarize, orally or in writing, the main points of the previous class meeting." Your summary may be inaccurate, but you will learn from the attempt.

On the other hand, some of the suggestions may require further understanding on your part. Consider Idea #4: "Become a questioner. Engage yourself in lectures and discussions by asking questions. If you don't ask questions, you will probably not discover what you do and do not know." In this case you may need to read further in the guide to get ideas of kinds of questions you can and should ask.

We suggest, therefore, that you employ a two-fold process. First, using **18 Ideas For Becoming A Master Student**, compile a personal list of suggestions or strategies you can immediately use. USE THEM IMMEDIATELY. Second, read through the remaining pages one by one looking for further strategies, especially as you acquire insight into items on the initial list of 18 ideas.

For example, you may want to ask more questions in class, but are not sure what to ask. Then, you read about eight basic structures in thinking: purpose, question, information, interpretation, concept, assumption, implication, and point of view. Each of the structures suggests to you possible questions. You then begin to pose some of them in class (Do chemists assume that...?).

Of course, this presupposes that you summon up the courage to raise your hand in class and actually ask questions (questions which your classmates may think odd). For example, you might raise your hand and say, "I was a little confused by chapter III in our text. What is the main idea of the chapter, as you see it?" If you just sit there afraid of what the other students might think, you will probably not ask any questions at all.

Finally, as you successfully implement some of the suggestions, your confidence and motivation should improve. Re-cycling through the guide, again and again, re-thinking what you are and are not doing, should raise you to yet further achievements as a student—a student seeking mastery.

Contents

Part I: Laying the Foundation

Part II: Following Through

18 Ideas for Becoming a Master Student

Idea #1: Make sure you thoroughly understand the requirements of each class, how it will be taught, and what will be expected of you. Ask questions about the grading policies and for advice on how best to prepare for class.

Idea #2: Become an active learner. Be prepared to work ideas into your thinking by active reading, writing, speaking, and listening.

Idea #3: Think of each subject you study as a form of thinking. (If you are in a history class, your goal should be to think historically; in a chemistry class to think chemically; etc.)

Idea #4: Become a questioner. Engage yourself in lectures and discussions by asking questions. If you don't ask questions, you will probably not discover what you do and do not know.

Idea #5: Look for interconnections. The content in every class is always a SYSTEM of interconnected ideas, never a random list of things to memorize. Don't memorize like a parrot. Study like a detective, always relating new learning to previous learning.

Idea #6: Think of your instructor as your coach. Think of yourself as a team member trying to practice the thinking exemplified by your instructor. For example, in an algebra class, think of yourself as going out for the algebra team and your teacher as demonstrating how to prepare for the games (tests).

Idea #7: Think about the textbook as the thinking of the author. Your job is to think the thinking of the author. For example, role play the author frequently. Explain the main points of the text to another student, as if you were the author.

Idea #8: Consider class time as a time in which you PRACTICE thinking (within the subject) using the fundamental concepts and principles of the course. Don't sit back passively, waiting for knowledge to fall into your head like rain into a rain barrel. It won't.

Idea #9: Relate content whenever possible to issues and problems and practical situations in your life. If you can't connect it to life, you don't know it.

Idea #10: Figure out what study and learning skills you are not good at. Practice those skills whenever possible. Recognizing and correcting your weaknesses is a strength.

Idea #11: Frequently ask yourself: "Can I explain this to someone not in class?" (If not, then you haven't learned it well enough.)

Idea #12: Seek to find the key concept of the course during the first couple of class meetings. For example, in a biology course, try explaining what biology is in your own words. Then relate that definition to each segment of what you learn afterward. Fundamental ideas are the basis for all others.

Idea #13: Routinely ask questions to fill in the missing pieces in your learning. Can you elaborate further on this? Can you give an example of that? If you don't have examples, you are not connecting what you are learning to your life.

Idea #14: Test yourself before you come to class by trying to summarize, orally or in writing, the main points of the previous class meeting. If you cannot summarize main points, you haven't learned them.

Idea #15: Learn to test your thinking using intellectual standards. "Am I being clear? Accurate? Precise? Relevant? Logical? Am I looking for what is most significant?"

Idea #16: Use writing as a way to learn by writing summaries in your own words of important points from the textbook or other reading material. Make up test questions. Write out answers to your own questions.

Idea #17: Frequently evaluate your listening. Are you actively listening for main points? Can you summarize what your instructor is saying in your own words? Can you elaborate what is meant by key terms?

Idea #18: Frequently evaluate your reading. Are you reading the text book actively? Are you asking questions as you read? Can you distinguish what you understand from what you don't?

How to Study and Learn a Discipline

The Problem:

All thinking occurs within, and across, disciplines and domains of knowledge and experience, yet few students learn how to think well within those domains. Despite having taken many classes, few are able to think biologically, chemically, geographically, sociologically, anthropologically, historically, artistically, ethically, or philosophically. Students study literature, but do not think in a literary way as a result. They study poetry, but do not think poetically. They do not know how to think like a reader when reading, nor how to think like a writer while writing, nor how to think like a listener while listening. Consequently they are poor readers, writers, and listeners. They use words and ideas, but do not know how to think ideas through, and internalize foundational meanings. They take classes but cannot make connections between the logic of a discipline and what is important in life. Often even the best students have these deficiencies.

A Definition:

Critical thinking is the kind of thinking—about any subject, content, or domain—that improves itself through disciplined analysis and assessment. Analysis requires knowledge of the elements of thought; assessment requires knowledge of standards for thought.

The Solution:

To study well and learn any subject is to learn how to think with discipline within that subject. It is to learn to think within its logic, to:

- raise vital questions and problems within it, formulating them clearly and precisely;
- gather and assess information, using ideas to interpret that information insightfully;
- come to well-reasoned conclusions and solutions, testing them against relevant criteria and standards;
- adopt the point of view of the discipline, recognizing and assessing, as need be, its assumptions, implications, and practical consequences;
- communicate effectively with others using the language of the discipline and that of educated public discourse; and
- relate what one is learning in the subject to other subjects and to what is significant in human life.

To become a skilled learner is to become a self-directed, self-disciplined, self-monitored, and self-corrective thinker, who has given assent to rigorous standards of thought and mindful command of their use. Skilled learning of a discipline requires that one respect its power as well as its limitations.

> **Essential Idea: The skills of critical thinking are the keys to learning every subject.**

          www.criticalthinking.org

How To Learn With Discipline

When learning: look for <u>interrelationships,</u> try to connect everything together. Think of learning as figuring out the parts of an organized and intelligible **system** (with everything fitting together like the parts of a jig-saw puzzle).

Everything you learn is related to every other thing you learn and learning things in relation to each other makes everything you learn more memorable, more intelligible, and more useful. Understanding science is understanding the "system" that scientific thinking represents. Understanding grammar is understanding the "system" that grammatical thinking represents. In other words, there is a logic to science, a logic to grammar, a logic to everything whatsoever! Science is about scientific thinking, grammar is about grammatical thinking, psychology is about psychological thinking, and so on.

In grammar, nouns (having something to talk about) make no sense without verbs (saying something about them). At the same time, to use nouns (and hence talk about something) successfully you need adjectives (to qualify them). To use verbs successfully you need adverbs (to qualify them). Each grammatical structure plays a logical role in a system of meaningful relationships—which one understands best as an interrelated system of ideas.

All "content" is logically interdependent. To understand one part of some content requires that you figure out its relation to other parts of that content. For example, you understand what a scientific experiment is only when you understand what a scientific theory is. You understand what a scientific theory is only when you understand what a scientific hypothesis is. You understand what a scientific hypothesis is only when you understand what a scientific prediction is. You understand what a scientific prediction is only when you understand what it is to scientifically test a view. You understand what it is to scientifically test a view only when you understand what a scientific experiment is, etc. To learn any body of content, therefore, is to figure out (i.e., reason or think through) the connections between the parts of that content. There is no learning of the content without this thinking process.

> **Essential Idea:** When learning any concept, idea, law, theory, or principle, ask yourself: To what other concepts, ideas, laws, theories, or principles is this connected?

How to Identify an Underlying Idea for the Subjects You Study

Virtually all courses have some inherent unity which, when understood, ties all the learning of the course together (like a tapestry). This unity is typically found in foundational ideas that define the subject and its goals. Below are suggestions for beginning to understand the foundational ideas behind some of the major disciplines. Use them to begin to think within the subjects. However, you must make sure you can state, elaborate, exemplify, and illustrate each of these ideas IN YOUR OWN WORDS with your own examples and illustrations. Otherwise, you are merely mouthing words that have no definite meaning in your mind.

- **Mathematics** as learning to think quantitatively
- **Economics** as the study of "who gets what, when, and how"
- **Algebra** as arithmetic with unknowns
- **Sociology** as the study of human conformity to group norms
- **Anthropology** as the physical and historical study of humans in light of their evolution from non-cultural into cultural animals
- **Physics** as the study of mass and energy and their interaction
- **Chemistry** as the study of elementary substances and the manner in which they react with each other
- **Philosophy** as the study of ultimate questions with a view to living an examined life
- **Biochemistry** as the chemistry of life processes in plants and animals
- **Science** as the attempt to learn through quantifiable observations and controlled experimentation
- **Theology** as the study of theories of spiritual reality
- **Ethics** as the study of principles to be used in contributing to the good of, and avoiding unnecessary harm to, humans and other sentient creatures
- **Art** as the application of skill and judgment to matters of taste and beauty (as in poetry, music, painting, dance, drama, sculpture, or architecture)
- **Professions** as ways of earning a living through the skilled and artful use of knowledge in everyday life

> **Essential Idea: When beginning to learn a subject, it is helpful to formulate an organizing idea to guide your thinking.**

Understanding Content Through The Thinking It Requires:
A Key To Deep Learning

All Subjects Represent A Systematic Way of Thinking. The first and most important insight necessary for deep learning of academic subjects is that everything you learn is, in the last analysis, nothing more nor less than a systematic way of thinking about a particular set of things.

Organized Systematically by Ideas. There is no way to learn a body of content without learning the ideas that define and structure it. There is no way to learn a concept without learning how to use it in thinking something through. Hence, to learn the idea of democracy is to learn how to figure out whether some group is functioning democratically or not. To learn the idea of fair play is to learn how to figure out whether someone is being fair in the manner in which they are participating in a game. To learn the idea of a novel is to learn how to distinguish a novel from a play or short story. To learn the idea of a family is to learn how to distinguish a family from a gang or club. To learn any body of content, therefore, it is necessary to learn to think accurately and reasonably within the ideas that define the content.

Leading to a Systematic Way of Questioning. Ideas within a subject are intimately connected with the kind of questions asked in it. All subjects represent ways of asking and answering a body of questions. There is no way to learn mathematical content without learning how to figure out correct answers to mathematical questions and problems. There is no way to learn historical content without learning how to figure out correct or reasonable answers to historical questions and problems. There is no way to learn biological content without learning how to figure out answers to biological questions and problems. We study chemistry to figure out chemicals (to answer questions about chemicals). We study sociology to figure out people (how and why people behave as they do in groups). All subjects can be understood in this way.

Essential Idea: All subjects represent a systematic way of thinking defined by a system of ideas leading to a distinctive and systematic way of questioning.

How to Identify the Structure of a Subject:
The Elements of Thought

The Elements of Thought: There are eight basic structures present in all thinking: Whenever we think, we think for a purpose within a point of view based on assumptions leading to implications and consequences. We use ideas and theories to interpret data, facts, and experiences in order to answer questions, solve problems, and resolve issues. In other words, all thinking within a discipline:

- **generates purposes**
- **raises questions**
- **uses information**
- **utilizes concepts**
- **makes inferences**
- **makes assumptions**
- **generates implications**
- **embodies a point of view**

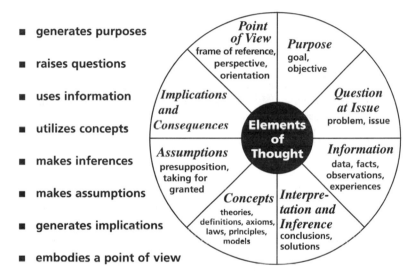

Each of these structures has implications for the others. Change your purpose or agenda, you change your questions and problems. Change your questions and problems, you are forced to seek new information and data. Collect new information and data... If you want to learn to think within a discipline, you must become deeply familiar with each of these structures. You should look for these structures as you learn: in lectures, discussions, textbooks, concepts, laws, theories...

> **Essential Idea: There are eight structures that define thinking. Learning to analyze thinking requires practice in identifying these structures in use.**

How to Figure Out the Form of Thinking Essential to Courses or Subjects

Consider the following thinking on the part of a student taking a course in history:

> *"To do well in this course, I must begin to think historically. I must not read the textbook as a bunch of disconnected stuff to remember but as the thinking of the historian. I must myself begin to think like a historian. I must begin to be clear about historical purposes (What are historians trying to accomplish?). I must begin to ask historical questions (and recognize the historical questions being asked in the lectures and textbook). I must begin to sift through historical information, drawing some historical conclusions. I must begin to question where historical information comes from. I must notice the historical interpretations that the historian forms to give meaning to historical information. I must question those interpretations (at least sufficiently to understand them). I must begin to question the implications of various historical interpretations and begin to see how historians reason to their conclusions. I must begin to look at the world as historians do, to develop a historical viewpoint. I will read each chapter in the textbook looking explicitly for the elements of thought in that chapter. I will actively ask (historical) questions in class from the critical thinking perspective. I will begin to pay attention to my own historical thinking in my everyday life. I will try, in short, to make historical thinking a more explicit and prominent part of my thinking."*

Students who approach history classes as historical thinking begin to understand the historical dimension of other subjects as well. For example, they begin to recognize that every subject itself has a history and that the present state of the subject is a product of its historical evolution. What is more, such historically-thinking students also notice the overlap between history as a study of the relatively recent past of humans (the last 30,000 years) and the much longer history of humans (canvassed in anthropology). They are able to place these last 30,000 years (which seem a long time when we first think of it) into the larger historical perspective of anthropology which begins its study of the human past some 2,000,000 years ago when our ancestors were small, hairy, apelike creatures who used tools such as digging sticks and clubs, walked upright, carried their tools, and lived on plant food. What is more, they see this longer history breaking down into stages: from hunting and gathering civilizations to agricultural civilizations to industrial civilizations to post-industrial civilizations.

And that is not all. They are then able to take this historical perspective and put it into a yet larger historical view by shifting from anthropological thinking to geographical thinking. They grasp that human history is itself a small part of a much older history, that of mammals, and that the age of mammals was preceded by an age of reptiles, and that by the age of coal-plants, and that by the age of fish, and that by the age of mollusks. They then can take the next step and grasp that geological history, even though reaching back thousands of millions of years is comparatively short when compared to that of the solar system, while that of the solar system is comparatively short when compared to the galaxy, while that of the galaxy is comparatively short when compared to the universe itself.

Students' capacity to think historically in larger and larger time spans continues to develop as their study of all subjects is transformed by a developing sense of the drama of time itself. They are then able to shift from history to pre-history, from pre-history to anthropological history, from anthropological history to geological history, and from geological history to astronomical history. In this ever-expanding perspective, the history of human knowledge is pitifully short: a milli-second geologically, a milli-milli second astronomically. It is only a second ago—astronomically speaking—that a species has emerged, Homo sapiens, which drives itself, and creates the conditions to which it itself must then adapt in new and unpredictable ways. It is only a milli-second ago that we have developed the capacity, though not the propensity, to think critically.

> **Essential Idea: It is possible to think deeply within a subject and see applications of that thinking in related subjects. Doing so increases the power of thinking and learning.**

How to Think Within the Ideas of a Subject

Learning to think within the ideas of a subject is like learning to perform well in basketball, ballet, or on the piano. Thinking within the ideas of a subject at an advanced level without disciplined practice is as unnatural to the human mind as sitting down at a piano and spontaneously playing Chopin's Polonaise.

Unfortunately, many classes do not highlight how to think within the ideas of the subject. Merely receiving lectures on the content of a subject will not teach you how to think within its ideas. You must therefore set out to discover how to think within biology, how to think within chemistry, how to think within economics, etc. You will not discover this thinking by cramming large masses of partially digested contents of a textbook or sets of lectures into your head. Here is what we recommend.

Recognize that you are seeking a new way to look at learning. Recognize that it will take time to become comfortable in this new perspective. Consider your task as a student to be to learn new ways to think. Stretching the mind to accommodate new ideas is crucial.

For example, if you are in a history course, your job is to learn how to think historically. If you are in a writing class, your job is to learn to think like a skilled writer. If you are in a sociology, psychology, geography, biology, philosophy, or chemistry class, you should be striving to think sociologically, psychologically, geographically, biologically, philosophically, or chemically.

If you are in a nursing, engineering, or architecture class, you should be attempting to think like a professional nurse, like an engineer, or like an architect.

Recognize that there are key ideas behind the subject that give a unified meaning to it. Look up a variety of formulations of the essence of the subject (use dictionaries, textbooks, encyclopedias). Remember that you are looking for the ideas that give a unified meaning to the subject and thus enable you to experience the subject as a system. What makes art art? What makes science science? What makes biology biology? Try to find the common denominator of the subjects you study. Ask your instructor for help.

Now relate every new idea (in the textbook or lectures) to the fundamental idea with which you began. The big idea with which you began should be in the background of all new ideas. Seek intuitive connections, connections that make complete sense to you.

> **Essential Idea: There are basic ideas that act as guide-posts to all thinking within a subject. Look for these basic ideas and stretch your mind to learn them. Weave everything else into them.**

How to Analyze the Logic of an Article, Essay, or Chapter

One important way to understand an essay, article, or chapter, is through the analysis of the parts of the author's reasoning. Once you have done this, you can then evaluate the author's reasoning using intellectual standards (see page 32). Here is a template to follow:

1) The main **purpose** of this article is _____.
   (Here you are trying to state, as accurately as possible, the author's purpose for writing the article. What was the author trying to accomplish?)

2) The key **question** that the author is addressing is _____. (Your goal is to figure out the key question that was in the mind of the author when s/he wrote the article. In other words, what was the key question that the article addressed?)

3) The most important **information** in this article is _____. (You want to identify the key information the author used, or presupposed, in the article to support his/her main arguments. Here you are looking for facts, experiences, and/or data the author is using to support her/his conclusions.)

4) The main **inferences**/conclusions in this article are _____
   _____.
   (You want to identify the most important conclusions that the author comes to and presents in the article).

5) The key **idea**(s) we need to understand in this article is (are)_____. By these ideas the author means_____.
   (To identify these ideas, ask yourself: What are the most important ideas that you would have to understand in order to understand the author's line of reasoning? Then briefly elaborate what the author means by these ideas.)

6) The main **assumption**(s) underlying the author's thinking is (are)_____ (Ask yourself: What is the author taking for granted [that might be questioned]. The assumptions are generalizations that the author does not think s/he has to defend in the context of writing the article, and they are usually unstated. This is where the author's thinking logically begins.)

7) a)If we take this line of reasoning seriously, the **implications** are _____.
(What consequences are likely to follow if people take the author's line of reasoning seriously? Here you are to follow out the logical implications of the author's position. You should include implications that the author states, but also include those that the author does not state.)

7)b) If we fail to take this line of reasoning seriously, the **implications** are _____.
(What consequences are likely to follow if people ignore the author's reasoning?)

8) The main **point(s) of view** presented in this article is (are) _____. (The main question you are trying to answer here is: What is the author looking at, and how is s/he seeing it? For example, in this mini-guide we are looking at "education" and seeing it "as involving the development of intellectual skills." We are also looking at "learning" as "the responsibility of students.")

If you truly understand these structures as they interrelate in an article, essay, or chapter, you should be able to empathically role-play the thinking of the author. Remember, these are the eight basic structures that define all reasoning. They are the essential elements of thought.

Essential Idea: Use the basic structures of thinking to analyze articles, essays, and chapters.

How to Figure Out the Logic of a Textbook

Just as you can understand an essay, article, or chapter is by analyzing the parts of the author's reasoning, so can you figure out the system of ideas within a textbook by focusing on the parts of the author's reasoning within the textbook. To understand the parts of the textbook author's reasoning, use this template:

The Logic of a Textbook

1) The main **purpose** of this textbook is _____.
(Here you are trying to determine the author's purpose for writing the textbook. What was the author trying to accomplish?)

2) The key **question**(s) that the author is addressing in the textbook is_____.
(You are trying to figure out the key question that was in the mind of the author when s/he wrote the textbook, in other words, What was the key question which the textbook answers? Here, you might identify the most broad question the textbook answers, along with the most important sub questions it focuses on.)

3) The most important kinds of **information** in this textbook are _____. (You want to identify the types of information the author uses in the textbook to support his/her main arguments [e.g., research results, observations, examples, experience, etc.].)

4) The main **inferences**/conclusions in this textbook are _____. (You want to identify the most important conclusions that the author comes to and presents in the text book. Focus on this question: What are the most important conclusions that the author presents, conclusions that, if you understand them, shed important light on key beliefs in the field?)

5) The key **idea**(s) we need to understand in this textbook is (are) _____. By these ideas the author means _____.

(To identify these ideas, ask yourself: What are the most important ideas that you would have to understand in order to understand the textbook? Then elaborate on precisely what the author means by these basic ideas. Begin with the most fundamental idea presented such as "science, biology, psychology, etc." These can usually be found in the first chapter. Then identify the other significant concepts that are deeply tied into the most fundamental one.)

6) The main <u>assumption</u>(s) underlying the author's thinking is (are) _____. (Ask yourself: What is the author taking for granted [that might be questioned]? The assumptions are sometimes generalizations that the author does not think s/he has to defend in the context of writing the textbook. The assumptions are sometimes stated in the first chapter as the key assumptions underlying the subject area.)

7) a) If people take the textbook seriously, the <u>implications</u> are _____.

(What consequences are likely to follow if readers take the text book seriously? Here you are to follow out the logical implications of the information/ideas in the textbook. You should include implications that the author argues for, if you believe them to be well-founded, but you should also include unstated implications as well.)

7) b) If people fail to take the textbook seriously, the <u>implications</u> are _____. (What consequences are likely to follow if the author's thinking is ignored in a situation when it is relevant?)

8) The main <u>point(s) of view</u> presented in this article is (are) _____. (The main question you are trying to answer here is: What is the author looking at, and how is s/he seeing it? For example, the author might be looking at "science" and seeing it as "the most effective tool for better understanding the physical world and how it operates.")

> **Essential Idea: Use the basic structure of thinking to analyze the thinking implicit in textbooks.**

How to Understand Ideas

Ideas are to us like the air we breathe. We project them everywhere. Yet we rarely notice this. We use ideas to create our way of seeing things. What we experience we experience through ideas, often funneled into the categories of "good" and "evil." We assume ourselves to be good. We assume our enemies to be evil. We select positive terms to cover up the indefensible things we do. We select negative terms to condemn even the good things our enemies do. We conceptualize things <u>personally</u> by means of experience unique to ourselves (often distorting the world to our advantage). We conceptualize things <u>socially</u> as a result of indoctrination or social conditioning (our allegiances presented, of course, in positive terms).

Ideas, then, are our paths to both reality and self-delusion. We don't typically recognize ourselves as engaged in idea construction of any kind whether illuminating or distorting. In our everyday life we don't experience ourselves shaping what we see and constructing the world to our advantage.

To the uncritical mind, it is as if people in the world came to us with our labels for them inherent in who they are. THEY are "terrorists." WE are "freedom fighters." All of us fall victims at times to an inevitable illusion of objectivity. Thus we see others not as like us in a common human nature, but as "friends" and "enemies," and accordingly "good" or "bad". Ideology, self-deception, and myth play a large part in our identity and how we think and judge. We apply ideas, however, as if we were simply neutral observers of reality. We often become self-righteous when challenged.

If you want to develop as a learner, you must come to recognize the ideas through which you see and experience the world. You must take explicit command of your thinking. You must become the master of your own ideas. You must learn how to think with alternative ideas, alternative "world views." As general semanticists often say: "The word is not the thing! The word is not the thing!" If you are trapped in one set of concepts (ideas, words) then your thinking is trapped. Word and thing become one and the same in your minds. You are unable then to act as a truly free person.

> **Essential Idea: To understand our experience and the world itself, we must be able to think within alternative world views. We must question our ideas. We must not confuse our words or ideas with things.**

How to Control (and Not Be Controlled By) Ideas

The ideas we have formed in personal experience are often egocentric in nature. The ideas we inherit from social indoctrination are typically ethnocentric in nature. Both can significantly limit our insight. This is where mastery of academic subjects and of our native language comes into play. This is where education is supposed to empower us.

The ideas we learn from academic subjects and from the study of distinctions inherent in language-use represent sources of ideas that can take us beyond our personal egocentrism and the social ideology in which we are otherwise typically entrapped. When we learn to think historically, sociologically, anthropologically, scientifically, and philosophically, we can come to see ignorance, prejudice, stereotypes, illusions, and biases in our personal thinking and in the thinking common in our society. Many, without such command, confuse very different things: for example, <u>needing</u> and <u>wanting</u>, <u>having judgment</u> and <u>being judgmental</u>, <u>having information</u> and <u>gaining knowledge</u>, <u>being humble</u> and <u>being servile</u>, being <u>stubborn</u> and <u>having the courage of one's convictions.</u>

Command of distinctions such as these and those inherent in multiple disciplines can have a significant influence upon the way we shape our experience. If, for example, we confuse ethics with arbitrary social conventions or religion or national law, we have no basis for understanding the true basis of universality in ethics: awareness of what does harm or good to humans and other sentient creatures.

When we develop our thinking, we go beneath the surface of ideas. Our personal experience is no longer "sacred." We recognize our fallibility. We strive for ideas to broaden and empower us as free individuals.

> **Essential Idea:** There are at least four different sources for ideas: our personal experience, socialization, the academic subjects we study, and our native language (English, Spanish, etc.) To become truly educated, we must learn to monitor and evaluate our use of ideas from these domains. Only then can we learn how to control (and not be controlled by) ideas.

How to Understand Reading, Writing, Speaking, Listening and Thinking

Reading, writing, speaking, and listening are important to your success as a student. For example, if you are truly a skilled reader, you can master a subject from a textbook alone, without benefit of lectures or class discussion. Many excellent readers have become educated persons through reading alone. Abraham Lincoln is one such person.

Or consider writing. The art of writing well forces us to make explicit what we do and do not understand. Often we have the illusion we understand an idea—until we try to express our understanding in written form. Suddenly, we see problems. We discover the subject is more complex than we thought. Writing to learn is a powerful tool in learning deeply and well. Get in the habit of writing as a tool in learning.

Speaking is another powerful tool in learning. If we can explain what we are learning to another person, we typically gain a deeper level of understanding ourselves. This is why we have the saying that "in teaching you will learn." Entering into an oral dialogue with other learners is a powerful tool in learning. Speaking clearly and precisely about what we are learning solidifies our understanding. Seek occasions to give voice to what you are learning.

Listening well is probably the least understood of the four modalities of communication we are considering. Much human listening is passive, associational, uncritical, and superficial. Poor listening leads not only to incomplete internalization, but also to blatant misunderstanding.

It is important to recognize that reading, writing, speaking, and listening are all modes of thinking. Your primary goal as a student should be to learn how to read, write, speak, and listen well. Happily, these four different modes of thinking are deeply interrelated, and learning how to take charge of one is significantly related to learning to take charge of the other three.

For example, irrespective of whether you are reading, writing, speaking, or listening it is important to be clear, precise, accurate, relevant, responsive to complexity, broad as the issue requires, and focused on the appropriate point(s) of view. Here are some suggestions:

1. **Reading:** Get in the habit of reading both "closely" and "structurally." Close reading: stop after every paragraph to summarize, either orally or in writing, what is being said. You might get into the habit of explicitly stating the "essential idea" in a passage, as we have done throughout this mini-guide. Structural reading: Read closely the table of contents as well as any introductory sections. Then summarize, either orally or in writing, the basic ideas—the big ideas—behind the book. Structural reading gives you perspective (a picture of the whole), thus enabling you to decide where to focus your close reading.

2. **Writing:** Get in the habit of writing summaries of basic ideas and their interconnections. Read and explain what you have written to others.

3. **Speaking:** Get in the habit of explaining what you are learning to others. The better you are at explaining something, the better you understand it.

4. **Listening:** Get in the habit of questioning those to whom you are listening. Role-play their point of view. Ask for correction. The better you can express the thoughts of another, the better you will understand them.

> **Essential Idea: Reading, writing, speaking, and listening are all modes of thinking. Each is important to your success as a student. Take the time to develop your reading, writing, speaking, and listening skills.**

How to Learn Ideas from Textbooks

■ All textbooks are organized by systems of ideas within them. Diagram the systems to help you begin to learn them. Notice yourself naming, identifying, connecting, distinguishing, and explaining things using ideas.

■ Where we have knowledge, we have an organized technical vocabulary. Create a glossary of the most important ideas you learn in each subject you study.

■ Your knowledge can be no stronger than the knowledge you have of ideas in a subject. Test yourself by trying to explain key ideas in non-technical language.

■ All ideas must be understood in relation to contrasting ideas. Try naming and explaining the ideas opposite to key ideas you learn.

■ All idea clusters must be understood as part of further such clusters. Take any important idea you learn and name the ideas that cluster around it.

■ There are many domains of ideas: ethical, religious, cultural social, political, scientific, mathematical, etc. Name and explain a key idea in each domain.

■ At the beginning of each semester, try making a list of at least 25 ideas you want to learn in each subject. To do this you might read an introductory chapter from the textbook or an article on each subject from an encyclopedia. Then explain the list of ideas to a friend (state, elaborate, exemplify, and illustrate each).

■ As the course proceeds, add new ideas to the list and underline those ideas you are confident you can explain. Regularly translate chapter and section titles from the textbook into ideas. In addition, look for key ideas in every lecture you hear. Relate basic ideas to the basic theory the subject uses to solve problems. Master fundamental ideas and theories well. Do not move on until you do.

Essential Idea: One important way to think about what you are learning is by highlighting, diagramming, and explaining the ideas at the heart of each subject you study.

Part II: Following Through

In the following section are ideas and strategies that build on those of Part I. Begin by testing yourself on your use of the recommendations with which this guide began. Remember, this guide can help you only if you are following its recommendations and thus developing habits based on them. There is no magic to developing powerful study habits just knowledge and hard work.

How Good a Student Are You Now? Test Yourself

How to Think Through the Defining Traits of the Disciplined Mind

How to Understand Intellectual Standards

How to Question Using Intellectual Standards

How to Evaluate an Author's Reasoning

How to Raise Important Questions Within a Subject

How to Distinguish One-System from
Competing-Systems Disciplines

How to Ask Questions About Fields of Study

How to Ask Questions About Textbooks

How to Understand the Logic of Biochemistry (An Example)

How to Think Biologically (An Example)

How to Think Historically (An Example)

How to Understand the Logic of Philosophy, Sociology
Psychology and Archaeology (Four Final Examples)

How to Understand the Role of Questions in Thinking and Learning

How to Distinguish Inert Information and Activated Ignorance
from Activated Knowledge

A Test to Repeat in Every Class and Subject

How Good a Student Are You?

Test Yourself:

#1: Do you understand the requirements of every class in which you are registered, how they will be taught, and what will be expected of you? Have you sought out and received advice about how you can best prepare for class?

#2: Do you know your strengths and weaknesses as a student and thinker? Have you tried to find out? Are you in the habit of evaluating aspects of your thinking—your purpose, the question you are trying to answer, the information you are using to answer it, etc.? Good thinkers regularly question their thinking. Be especially careful to distinguish what you know for sure from what you merely believe (but may not be true).

#3: Have you identified the KIND of thinking that is most important in a given class? Think of subjects as forms of thinking (history = historical thinking; sociology = sociological thinking; biology = biological thinking).

#4: Do you ask questions in and out of class? Do you engage yourself in lectures and discussions by asking questions? Good instructors value questions from students.

#5: Are you looking for interconnections? Do you understand the content in every class as a SYSTEM of interconnected understandings or as a random list of things to memorize? Don't memorize individual points like a parrot. Study to understand, to figure things out.

#6: Are you practicing the thinking of the subject? Could you explain this thinking with examples and illustrations (to someone who was not in the class)?

#7: Are you reading your textbooks to figure out the THINKING of the author(s)? Do you translate the author's thinking into your thinking (by putting basic points into your own words)? Do you role-play the author (to someone else) explaining the main points of the various sections of the text?

#8: Do you relate content whenever possible to issues and problems and practical situations in life? If you can't connect what you are learning to issues in life, your understanding of it is at best incomplete.

#9: Can you explain the main idea behind the class in your own words? Are you seeking to find the key concept of the course from the first couple of class meetings? For example, in a biology course, try explaining what biologists are (mainly) trying to figure out. Don't use technical terms in your explanation. Then relate that explanation to each segment of what you are learning in the course. How does each segment fit in?

#10: Do you test yourself before you come to class by trying to summarize, orally or in writing, the main points of the previous class meeting? If you cannot summarize main points, you haven't learned them.

#11: Do you check your thinking using intellectual standards? "Am I being clear? Accurate? Precise? Relevant? Logical? Am I looking for what is most significant? Am I recognizing complexities? "

#12: Do you use writing as a way to learn by writing summaries in your own words of important points from the textbook or other reading material? Do you make up test questions? Do you write out answers to your own questions?

#13: During lecture time, do you actively listen for main points? If we arbitrarily stopped the lecture at various points, could you accurately summarize what the instructor had just said in your own words?

#14: Do you frequently assess your reading? Do you read the textbook <u>actively</u>? Are you asking questions as you read? Do you recognize the points you do and do not understand?

Well, what do you think? How good a student are you?

How to Think Through the Defining Traits of the Disciplined Mind

As a student, you need to cultivate not only intellectual abilities, but intellectual dispositions as well. These attributes are essential to excellence of thought. They determine with what insight and integrity you think. Here we briefly describe the intellectual virtues and provide related questions that foster their development. *Only to the extent that you are routinely asking these questions of yourself are you developing these virtues.*

Intellectual humility is knowledge of ignorance, sensitivity to what you know and what you do not know. It means being aware of your biases, prejudices, self-deceptive tendencies, and the limitations of your viewpoint. Questions that foster intellectual humility include:

■ What do I really know (about myself, about the situation, about another person, about my nation, about what is going on in the world)?

■ To what extent do my prejudices or biases influence my thinking?

■ To what extent have I been indoctrinated into beliefs that may be false?

■ How do the beliefs I have uncritically accepted keep me from seeing things as they are?

Intellectual courage is the disposition to question beliefs you feel strongly about. It includes questioning the beliefs of your culture and the groups to which you belong, and a willingness to express your views even when they are unpopular. Questions that foster intellectual courage include:

■ To what extent have I analyzed the beliefs I hold?

■ To what extent have I questioned my beliefs, many of which I learned in childhood?

■ To what extent have I demonstrated a willingness to give up my beliefs when sufficient evidence is presented against them?

■ To what extent am I willing to stand up against the majority (even though people might ridicule me)?

Intellectual empathy is awareness of the need to actively entertain views that differ from our own, especially those we strongly disagree with. It is to accurately reconstruct the viewpoints and reasoning of our opponents and to reason from premises, assumptions, and ideas other than our own. Questions that foster intellectual empathy include:

■ To what extent do I accurately represent viewpoints I disagree with?

■ Can I summarize the views of my opponents to their satisfaction? Can I see insights in the views of others and prejudices in my own?

■ Do I sympathize with the feelings of others in light of their thinking differently than me?

Intellectual integrity consists in holding yourself to the same intellectual standards you expect others to honor (no double standards). Questions that foster intellectual integrity include:

- Do I behave in accordance with what I say I believe, or do I tend to say one thing and do another?
- To what extent do I expect the same of myself as I expect of others?
- To what extent are there contradictions or inconsistencies in my life?
- To what extent do I strive to recognize and eliminate self-deception in my life?

Intellectual perseverance is the disposition to work your way through intellectual complexities despite the frustration inherent in the task. Questions that foster intellectual perseverance include:

- Am I willing to work my way through complexities in an issue or do I tend to give up when I experience difficulty?
- Can I think of a difficult intellectual problem in which I have demonstrated patience and determination in working through the difficulties?
- Do I have strategies for dealing with complex problems?
- Do I expect learning to be easy or do I recognize the importance of engaging in challenging intellectual work?

Confidence in reason is based on the belief that one's own higher interests and those of humankind at large are best served by giving the freest play to reason. It means using standards of reasonability as the fundamental criteria by which to judge whether to accept or reject any belief or position. Questions that foster confidence in reason include:

- Am I willing to change my position when the evidence leads to a more reasonable position?
- Do I adhere to principles of sound reasoning when persuading others of my position or do I distort matters to support my position?
- Do I deem it more important to "win" an argument, or see the issue from the most reasonable perspective?
- Do I encourage others to come to their own conclusions or do I try to force my views on them?

Intellectual autonomy is thinking for oneself while adhering to standards of rationality. It means thinking through issues using one's own thinking rather than uncritically accepting the viewpoints of others. Questions that foster intellectual autonomy:

- To what extent am I a conformist?
- To what extent do I uncritically accept what I am told by my government, the media, my peers?
- Do I think through issues on my own or do I merely accept the views of others?
- Having thought through an issue from a rational perspective, am I willing to stand alone despite the irrational criticisms of others?

How to Understand Intellectual Standards

Reasonable people judge reasoning by intellectual standards. When you internalize these standards and explicitly use them in your thinking, your thinking becomes more clear, more accurate, more precise, more relevant, deeper, broader, and more fair. You should note that we focus here on a selection of standards. Others include credibility, sufficiency, reliability, practicality, etc. The questions that employ these standards are listed on the following page.

Clarity:
understandable, the meaning can be grasped

Accuracy:
free from errors or distortions, true

Precision:
exact to the necessary level of detail

Relevance:
relating to the matter at hand

Depth:
containing complexities and interrelationships

Breadth:
encompassing multiple viewpoints

Logic:
the parts make sense together, no contradictions

Significance:
focusing on the important, not trivial

Fairness:
Justifiable, not self-serving (not egocentric)

Clarity
Could you elaborate further?
Could you give me an example?
Could you illustrate what you mean?

Accuracy
How could we check on that?
How could we find out if that is true?
How could we verify or test that?

Precision
Could you be more specific?
Could you give me more details?
Could you be more exact?

Relevance
How does that relate to the problem?
How does that bear on the question?
How does that help us with the issue?

Depth
What factors make this a difficult problem?
What are some of the complexities of this question?
What are some of the difficulties we need to deal with?

Breadth
Do we need to look at this from another perspective?
Do we need to consider another point of view?
Do we need to look at this in other ways?

Logic
Does all this make sense together?
Does your first paragraph fit in with your last?
Does what you say follow from the evidence?

Significance
Is this the most important problem to consider?
Is this the central idea to focus on?
Which of these facts are most important?

Fairness
Are my selfish desires keeping me from being fair to others?
Am I sympathetically entering the viewpoints of others?
Am I putting views I oppose in their strongest form?

How to Evaluate an Author's Reasoning

1. Focusing on the author's **Purpose:** Is the purpose of the author well-stated or clearly implied? Is it justifiable?

2. Focusing on the key **Question** which the written piece answers: Is the question at issue well-stated (or clearly implied)? Is it clear and unbiased? Does the expression of the question do justice to the complexity of the matter at issue? Are the question and purpose directly relevant to each other?

3. Focusing on the most important **Information** presented by the author: Does the writer cite relevant evidence, experiences, and/or information essential to the issue? Is the information accurate and directly relevant to the question at issue? Does the writer address the complexities of the issue?

4. Focusing on the most fundamental **Concepts** which are at the heart of the author's reasoning: Does the writer clarify key ideas when necessary? Are the ideas used justifiably?

5. Focusing on the author's **Assumptions:** Does the writer show a sensitivity to what he or she is taking for granted or assuming? (Insofar as those assumptions might reasonably be questioned) Or does the writer use questionable assumptions without addressing problems inherent in those assumptions?

6. Focusing on the most important **Inferences** or conclusions in the written piece: Do the inferences and conclusions made by the author clearly follow from the information relevant to the issue, or does the author jump to unjustifiable conclusions? Does the author consider alternative conclusions where the issue is complex? In other words, does the author use a sound line of reasoning to come to logical conclusions, or can you identify flaws in the reasoning somewhere?

7. Focusing on the author's **Point of View:** Does the author show a sensitivity to alternative relevant points of view or lines of reasoning? Does s/he consider and respond to objections framed from other relevant points of view?

8. Focusing on **Implications:** Does the writer display a sensitivity to the implications and consequences of the position s/he is taking?

Essential Idea: You can evaluate thinking by applying intellectual standards to its component parts.

How to Raise Important Questions Within a Subject

Every discipline is best known by the questions it generates and the way it goes about settling those questions. To think well within a discipline, you must be able to raise and answer important questions within it. <u>At the beginning of a semester of study, try generating a list of at least 25 questions that each discipline you are studying seeks to answer.</u> To do this you might read an introductory chapter from the textbook or an article on the discipline from an encyclopedia. Then explain the significance of the questions to another person.

Then <u>add new questions to the list (as your courses proceed) underlining those questions when you are confident you can explain how to go about answering them. Regularly translate chapter and section titles from your textbooks into questions.</u> For example, a section on photosynthesis answers the question, What is photosynthesis?

In addition, <u>look for key questions in every lecture you hear. Relate basic questions to the basic theory the discipline uses to solve problems</u>. Master fundamental questions well. Do not move on until you understand them.

<u>Notice the interrelationship between key ideas and key questions.</u> Without the ideas the questions are meaningless. Without the questions, the ideas are inert. There is nothing you can do with them. A skilled thinker is able to take questions apart, generate alternative meanings, distinguish leading from subordinate questions, and grasp the demands that questions put upon us.

Essential Idea: If you become a good questioner within a discipline, you will learn the essential content of the discipline.

How to Distinguish One-System from Competing-Systems Disciplines

In some disciplines, the experts rarely disagree; in others, disagreement is common. The reason for this is found in the kinds of questions they ask and the nature of what they study. Mathematics and the physical and biological sciences fall into the first category. They study phenomena that behave consistently under predictable conditions and they pose questions that can be expressed clearly and precisely, with virtually complete expert agreement. The disciplines dealing with humans, in contrast—all the social disciplines, the Arts, and the Humanities—fall into the second category. What they study is often unpredictably variable. For example, humans are born into a culture at some point in time in some place, raised by parents with particular beliefs, and form a variety of associations with other humans who are equally variously influenced. What is dominant in our behavior varies from person to person. Hence, many of the questions asked in the disciplines dealing with human nature are subject to disagreement among experts (who approach the questions from different points of view). Consider the varieties of ways that human minds are influenced:

➢ sociologically (our minds are influenced by the social groups to which we belong);

➢ philosophically (our minds are influenced by our personal philosophy);

➢ ethically (our minds are influenced by our ethical character);

➢ intellectually (our minds are influenced by the ideas we hold, by the manner in which we reason and deal with abstractions);

➢ anthropologically (our minds are influenced by cultural practices, mores, and taboos);

➢ ideologically and politically (our minds are influenced by the structure of power and its use by interest groups around us);

➤ economically (our minds are influenced by the economic conditions under which we live);

➤ historically (our minds are influenced by our history and by the way we tell our history);

➤ biologically (our minds are influenced by our biology and neurology);

➤ theologically (our minds are influenced by our religious beliefs); and,

➤ psychologically (our minds are influenced by our personality and egocentric tendencies).

What is more, humans are capable of discovering how they are being influenced in these ways, may reflect on them, and then act to change their behavior in any number of ways. For example, consider how much more difficult it would be to study the behavior of mice if each mouse varied in its behavior from every other mouse depending on experience, personal philosophy, and culture. Or, consider what the study of the behavior of mice would be like if they could discover we were studying them and begin to react to our study in the light of that knowledge. And how could we even proceed to study them if they decided at the same time to study us studying them. In other words, the goal of studying human behavior faces enormous difficulties.

In studying a "one system" subject, in contrast, the task is to learn how to think within one overriding point of view. Learning to think algebraically, for example, does not require that you consider schools of thought within algebra. Algebraic thinking is based on a precisely defined system. Virtually all the ideas of algebra are shared by all mathematicians. Each idea is strictly and precisely defined. It is possible to PROVE this or that. Given a number system, one can derive arithmetic. Given arithmetic, one can derive algebra. Given algebra, one can derive calculus. All inferences can be tested, one by one.

> **Essential Idea:** For any subject one studies, it is important to know the extent of expert disagreement and the "variability" of what one is studying.

How to Ask Questions About Fields of Study

(Answer as many of these questions as you can by examining texts in the subject. You may need help from your instructor on some of them.)

1. To what extent are there competing schools of thought within this field?

2. To what extent do experts in this field disagree about the answers they give to important questions?

3. What other fields deal with this same subject (from a different standpoint, perhaps)? To what extent are there conflicting views about this subject in light of these different standpoints?

4. To what extent, if at all, is this field properly called a science?

5. To what extent can questions asked in the field be answered definitively? To what extent are questions in this field matters of (arguable) judgment?

6. To what extent is there public pressure on professionals in the field to compromise their professional practice in light of public prejudice or vested interest?

7. What does the history of the discipline tell you about the status of knowledge in the field? How old is the field? How common is controversy over fundamental terms, theories, and orientation?

Essential Idea: Many disciplines are not definitive in their pursuit of knowledge. As you learn a subject, it is important to understand both its strengths and limitations.

How to Ask Questions About Textbooks

(Answer as many of these questions as you can by examining your textbook. You may need help from your instructor on some of them.)

1. If there are competing schools of thought within this field, what is the orientation of the textbook writer(s)? Do they highlight these competing schools and detail the implications of that debate?

2. Are there other books available that approach this field from a significantly different standpoint? If there are, how should we understand the orientation or bias of this textbook?

3. Would other experts in this field disagree with any of the answers given in this textbook to important questions? How would they disagree?

4. Are there books in other fields that deal with this same subject (from a different standpoint, perhaps)? To what extent are there conflicting views about this subject in light of these different standpoints?

5. To what extent does this textbook represent this field as a science? If so, do some experts in the field disagree with this representation? In what sense is it not a science?

6. To what extent do the questions asked in this textbook lead to definitive answers? Conversely, to what extent are questions in this textbook matters of (arguable) judgment? And does the textbook help you to distinguish between these very different types of questions?

> **Essential Idea: Not all textbooks are equal as to quality. As you read a textbook, it is important to understand its strengths and limitations.**

How to Understand the Logic of Biochemistry (An Example)

Biochemical Goals. The goal of biochemistry is to determine the biological foundations of life through chemistry. Its aim is to use chemistry to study events on the scale of structures so small they are invisible even with a microscope.

Biochemical Questions. How do small-scale structures and events underlie the larger-scale phenomena of life? What chemical processes underlie living things? What is their structure? And what do they do? How can we correlate observations made at different levels of the organization of life (from the smallest to the largest)? How can we produce drugs that target undesirable events in living creatures?

Biochemical Information. The kinds of information biochemists seek are: information about the kind of chemical units out of which life is constructed, about the process by which key chemical reactions essential to the construction of life take place.

Biochemical Judgments. Biochemists seek to make judgments about the complex process of maintenance and growth of which life basically consists. In short, they seek to tell us how life functions at the chemical level.

Biochemical Ideas. There are a number of ideas essential to understanding biochemistry: the idea of levels of organization of life processes (molecular, sub-cellular particle, cellular, organ, and total organism), the idea of life structures and life processes, the idea of the dynamics of life, the idea of the unity of life processes amid a diversity of life forms, etc.

Biochemical Assumptions. Some of the key assumptions behind biochemical thinking are: that there are chemical foundations to life, that the techniques of chemistry are most fitting for the study of life at the level of molecules, that it is possible to use chemical ideas to explain life, that it is possible to analyze and discover the key agents in fundamental life process, and that it is possible, ultimately, to eliminate "unwanted" life processes while strengthening or maintaining desirable ones.

Biochemical Implications. The general implications of biochemistry are that we will increasingly be able to enhance human and other forms of life, and to diminish disease and other undesirable states, by application of chemical strategies.

Biochemical Point of View. The biochemical viewpoint sees the "chemical" level as revealing fundamental disclosures about the nature, function, and foundations of life. It sees chemistry as solving the most basic biological problems. It sees life processes at the chemical level to be highly unified and consistent, despite the fact that life process at the whole-animal level are highly diversified.

Essential Idea: When studying a subject, it is important to understand its basic logic. It is always possible to construct it, as in biochemistry.

How to Think Biologically (An Example)

Suppose you are taking a course in biology. Your goal is to practice biological thinking not to memorize the conclusions or interpretations of the textbook writer's thinking. Using introductory material, you write out the logic of biology (see biochemistry example).

You begin with the most basic idea of biology, the scientific study of living things (10,000,000 species) in fragile ecosystems. You discover that all biological thinking involves some account of the structure or function of living things and that life can be studied at different levels (molecule, organelle, cell, tissue, organ, organism, population, ecological community, and biosphere). You recognize that all forms of life reproduce, grow, and respond to changes in the environment. You begin to understand the intricate and often fragile relationship between all living things: that plants need animals and animals need plants. You come to recognize that all humans have an opportunity to live a better and fuller life if they understand life processes. You come to see that ignorance of ecological functions has led humans to destroy important environmental resources.

Thinking biologically you seek to understand how life works, the fundamental processes and ingredients of life. You soon recognize that all life forms, no matter how diverse, have common characteristics: 1) they are made up of cells, enclosed by a membrane that maintains internal conditions different from their surroundings, 2) they contain DNA or RNA as the material that carries their master plan, and 3) they carry out a process, called metabolism, which involves the conversion of different forms of energy through predictable chemical reactions. Linking chemical thinking to biological thinking, you come to recognize that life must first be understood on the chemical level, for it is at this level that strands of molecules of DNA produce cells, and ultimately, all forms of living things. The electronic relationships within atoms, you discover, account for the dynamics that drive internal processes and conditions of life.

Through "discoveries" and insights such as these your conception of biological thinking develops. You look for opportunities to discuss biological ideas with classmates and the instructor. You go to class armed with questions that you generate by reading your class notes and the textbook.

Essential Idea: When you begin to think biologically, you begin to see the connection of biological thinking to important human problems.

How To Think Historically (An Example)

Suppose you are taking a course in history. Your goal is to practice historical thinking and not to memorize the conclusions or interpretations of someone else's historical thinking (the contents of most history texts). You view the textbook as a product of historical thinking to be analyzed and assessed by your best attempt at historical thinking. You read to figure out the basic historical agenda of the professor and the textbook. You recognize that all historical thinking involves the construction of a story or account of the past with the purpose of enabling us to better understand the present.

You begin to see the connection of historical thinking in class and thinking in everyday life situations. You come to recognize that all humans engage in the act of creating their own story in the privacy of their minds, as well as in the light of the "stories" they hear others relating. You notice, for example, that gossip is a form of historical thinking (since we create stories about others while doing it). You notice that an issue of a daily newspaper is analogous to the writing of the history of yesterday (since the reporters and editors of a newspaper create accounts of what happened on the previous day).

You discover that for any given historical period, even one as short as a day, millions of events take place, with the implication that no given written history contains anything more than a tiny percentage of the total events which take place within any given historical period. You discover that historians must therefore regularly make value judgments to decide what to include in, and what to exclude from, their accounts. You learn that there are different possible stories and accounts that highlight different patterns in the events themselves: accounts that highlight "high-level" decision-makers (great person accounts), accounts that highlight different social and economic classes, different variables, different values, and different implications.

You learn that the specific questions that any given historical thinker asks depends on the specific agenda or goal of that thinker. You learn that it is the historical questions asked that determine which data or events are relevant.

You learn that one and the same event can be illuminated by different conceptualizations (for example, different political, social, and economic theories about people and social change). You learn that different historians make different assumptions that influence the way they frame their questions and the data that seem most important to them. You learn that when a given historian "identifies with" a given group of people and writes "their" history the resulting account often highlights the positive characteristics of those people and the negative characteristics of those with whom they were in conflict.

It is "discoveries" and insights such as these that shape your emerging conception of historical thinking and, therefore, of the nature of history itself. To practice your historical thinking you develop a brief account of your own personal history. You seek opportunities to express historical purposes, formulate historical questions and issues, gather or analyze historical data or information, make historical inferences, analyze historical ideas or theories, check historical assumptions, trace historical implications and consequences, and adopt historical viewpoints.

You look for opportunities to discuss historical problems or issues with classmates or the professor. You seek to gain historical insights into your own life. You go to class armed with questions (that you generate by reading your class notes and by reading the textbook). For example, on any given day you might ask any one or more of the following questions: What are we trying to accomplish in the way of historical thinking today? What kinds of historical questions are we asking? What kinds of historical problems are we trying to solve? What sort of historical information or data are we using? How can we get that information? What is the most basic historical idea, concept, or theory we are using? What am I learning today about historical thinking?

> **Essential Idea: When you begin to think historically, you begin to see the connection of historical thinking to everyday life situations.**

The Logic of Philosophy

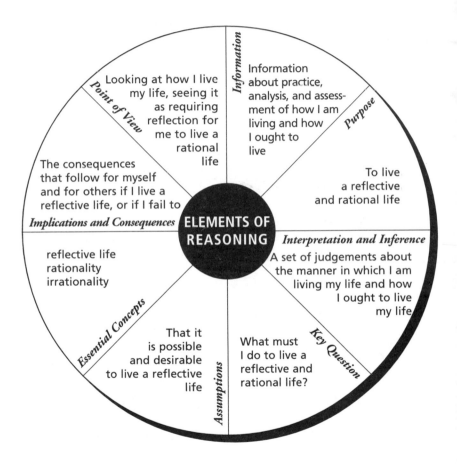

Information

Information about practice, analysis, and assessment of how I am living and how I ought to live

Point of View

Looking at how I live my life, seeing it as requiring reflection for me to live a rational life

Purpose

To live a reflective and rational life

The consequences that follow for myself and for others if I live a reflective life, or if I fail to

Implications and Consequences

ELEMENTS OF REASONING

Interpretation and Inference

A set of judgements about the manner in which I am living my life and how I ought to live my life

reflective life
rationality
irrationality

Essential Concepts

That it is possible and desirable to live a reflective life

Assumptions

What must I do to live a reflective and rational life?

Key Question

The Logic of Sociology

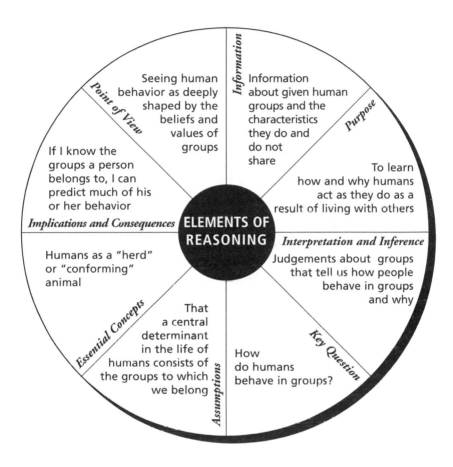

Point of View
Seeing human behavior as deeply shaped by the beliefs and values of groups

Information
Information about given human groups and the characteristics they do and do not share

Purpose
To learn how and why humans act as they do as a result of living with others

Implications and Consequences
If I know the groups a person belongs to, I can predict much of his or her behavior

ELEMENTS OF REASONING

Interpretation and Inference
Judgements about groups that tell us how people behave in groups and why

Humans as a "herd" or "conforming" animal

Essential Concepts
That a central determinant in the life of humans consists of the groups to which we belong

Assumptions

Key Question
How do humans behave in groups?

The Logic of Archaeology

- **Purpose of the Thinking:** The purpose of Archaeology is to find remnants of the past, interpreting and piecing them together in order to discover more about historical events, culture, and our human legacy.

- **Question at Issue:** What is the best way to find information about the distant past, and how does one effectively interpret the past through archaeology?

- **Information:** In order to become or think like an effective archaeologist, one should consider site discovery techniques, artifact retrieval, cataloging, and preservation techniques, contextual and cultural clues, and supportable historical and scientific data from archaeological finds.

- **Interpretation & Inference:** One must validate historical interpretations by cross-referencing various previous interpretations, current cultural evidence, and physical artifacts and scientific data from archaeological finds.

- **Concepts:** The concept of recovering lost history, of seeking evidence from beneath the surface of the earth to reveal important events and time sequences in ancient human history.

- **Assumptions:** We can always enrich our understanding of the past, and archaeology provides evidence to back-up theories. The past is a puzzle that can be further solved through ongoing archaeological study.

- **Implications & Consequences:** New discoveries that answer questions of the past can be made with on-going archaeological research. Beliefs we now hold as true, could one day be revised based on future discoveries. Understanding old ways of doing things could also provide the present or future with additional knowledge for interest or resources for survival.

- **Point of View:** Seeing the story of humankind as taking place through stages over hundreds of thousands of years.

How to Understand the Role of Questions in Thinking and Learning

Thinking is not driven by answers but by questions. Had no questions been asked by those who laid the foundation for a field—for example, physics or biology—the field would never have been developed in the first place. Furthermore, every field stays alive only to the extent that fresh questions are generated and taken seriously as the driving force in a process of thinking. To think through or rethink anything, one must ask questions that stimulate thought. Questions define tasks, express problems and delineate issues. Answers on the other hand, often signal a full stop in thought. Only when an answer generates a further question does thought continue its life as such. This is why it is only when you have questions that you are really thinking and learning.

So, instead of trying to store a lot of disconnected information in your mind, start asking questions about the content. Deep questions drive thought beneath the surface of things, forcing you to deal with complexity. Questions of purpose force you to define tasks. Questions of information force you to look at our sources of information as well as assess the quality of information. Questions of interpretation force you to examine how you are organizing or giving meaning to information. Questions of assumption force you to examine what you are taking for granted. Questions of implication force you to follow out where your thinking is going. Questions of point of view force you to examine your perspective and to consider other relevant view points.

Questions of relevance force you to discriminate what does and what does not bear on a question. Questions of accuracy force you to evaluate and test for truth and correctness. Questions of precision force you to give details and be specific. Questions of consistency force you to examine your thinking for contradictions. Questions of logic force you to consider how you are putting the whole of your thought together, to make sure that it all adds up and makes sense within a reasonable system of some kind.

Continually remind yourself that learning begins only when questions are asked.

> **Essential Idea: If you want to learn, you must ask questions that lead to further questions that lead to further questions. To question well is to learn well.**

How to Distinguish Inert Information and Activated Ignorance from Activated Knowledge

1) The mind can take in information in three distinctive ways: by internalizing inert information, by forming activated ignorance, and by achieving activated knowledge.

2) By <u>inert information</u>, we mean taking into the mind information that, though memorized, we do not understand. For example, many children learn in school that democracy is government of the people, by the people, for the people. But most people could not explain the difference between these three conditions. Much human information is, in the mind of the humans who possess it, merely empty words (inert or dead in the mind).

3) By <u>activated ignorance</u>, we mean taking into the mind, and actively using, information that is false. For example, the philosopher René Descartes came to confidently believe that animals have no actual feelings but are simply robotic machines. Based on this activated ignorance, he performed painful experiments on animals and interpreted their cries of pain as mere noises. Wherever activated ignorance exists, it is dangerous.

4) By <u>activated knowledge</u>, we mean taking into the mind, and actively using, information that is not only true but that, when insightfully understood, leads us by implication to more and more knowledge. For example, knowledge of critical thinking skills is activated knowledge when we use these skills over and over in the acquisition of knowledge. Knowing what a cell is in biology can be activated knowledge when we use that knowledge to better understand the structure of virtually every life form.

5) <u>Activated knowledge is the ultimate goal of all education.</u> When we have it, it transforms us. For example, when we truly recognize how social groups exercise control over our behavior, we bring a unique perspective to every social situation. We don't simply observe human behavior. We observe conformity, manipulation, and self-deception. Or again, when we recognize that the news media's goal is not public education but profit making, we are not surprised by their lack of global even-handedness. We realize that putting a reader-friendly spin on every story is a way to increase readership and sales.

6) <u>Activated knowledge is a key to lifelong learning.</u> In all subjects, seek the knowledge that can guide your thinking to further and further knowledge. Seek first principles. Seek basic laws and theories. Seek fundamental ideas. Use them as guideposts in learning.

Essential Idea: There are three very different ways to take in information:
1) in a way that it is meaningless to us,
2) in a misleading way, and
3) in a way that leads us to important knowledge through which we can acquire further knowledge and insight.

A Test to Repeat In Every Class and Subject

We have shown how every academic field has its own logic, or system of meanings. To learn the field is to learn the system. This is true whether one is talking of poems or essays, paintings or choreographed dances, histories or anthropological reports, experiments or scientific theories, philosophies or psychologies, particular events or general theories. Whether we are designing a new screwdriver or working out a perspective on religion, we must create a system of meanings that makes sense to us. To learn the system underlying a discipline is to create it in our mind. This requires that our thinking be re-shaped and modified. As you study a subject, periodically ask yourself:

"Can I explain the underlying system of ideas that defines this subject?" (This is like writing the encyclopedia entry for it.)

"Can I explain the most basic ideas in it to someone who doesn't understand it?" (Answering his/her questions about it.)

"Could I write a glossary of its most basic vocabulary (minimizing technical terms in my explanations of meaning)?"

"Do I understand the extent to which the subject involves a great deal of expert disagreement or very little expert disagreement?" (Competing-system vs. One-system fields.)

"Have I written out the basic logic of the subject?" (Its key purpose is...etc.)

"Can I compare and contrast the logic of the subject I am learning with that of other subjects I have learned?"

"To what extent can I relate this subject to significant problems in the world?"

"To what extent has thinking in this field helped me to become more intellectually humble, perseverant, autonomous...?"

The Thinker's Guide Series

The Thinker's Guide series provides convenient, inexpensive, portable references that students and faculty can use to improve the quality of studying, learning, and teaching. Their modest cost enables instructors to require them of all students (in addition to a textbook). Their compactness enables students to keep them at hand whenever they are working in or out of class. Their succinctness serves as a continual reminder of the most basic principles of critical thinking.

For Students & Faculty

Critical Thinking
The essence of critical thinking concepts and tools distilled into a 19-page pocket-size guide. (1-24 copies $4.00 each; 25-199 copies $2.00 each; 200-499 copies $1.75 each) #520m

How to Study & Learn
A variety of strategies—both simple and complex—for becoming not just a better student, but also a master student. (1-24 copies $6.00 each; 25-199 copies $4.00 each; 200-499 copies $2.50 each) #530m

Analytic Thinking
This guide focuses on the intellectual skills that enable one to analyze anything one might think about — questions, problems, disciplines, subjects, etc. It provides the common denominator between all forms of analysis. (1-24 copies $6.00 each; 25-199 copies $4.00 each; 200-499 copies $2.50 each) #595m

Scientific Thinking
The essence of scientific thinking concepts and tools. It focuses on the intellectual skills inherent in the well-cultivated scientific thinker. (1-24 copies $6.00 each; 25-199 copies $4.00 each; 200-499 copies $2.50 each) #590m

The Human Mind
Designed to give the reader insight into the basic functions of the human mind and to how knowledge of these functions (and their interrelations) can enable one to use one's intellect and emotions more effectively (1-24 copies $5.00 each; 25-199 copies $2.50 each; 200-499 copies $1.75 each) #570m

How to Detect Media Bias and Propaganda
Designed to help readers come to recognize bias in their nation's news and to recognize propaganda so that they can reasonably determine what media messages need to be supplemented, counter-balanced or thrown out entirely. It focuses on the internal logic of the news as well as societal influences on the media. (1-24 copies $6.00 each; 25-199 copies $4.00 each; 200-499 copies $2.50 each) #575m

Asking Essential Questions
Introduces the art of asking essential questions. It is best used in conjunction with the Miniature Guide to Critical Thinking and the How to Study mini-guide. (1-24 copies $6.00 each; 25-199 copies $4.00 each; 200-499 copies $2.50 each) #580m

Foundations of Ethical Reasoning
Provides insights into the nature of ethical reasoning, why it is so often flawed, and how to avoid those flaws. It lays out the function of ethics, its main impediments, and its social counterfeits. (1-24 copies $6.00 each; 25-199 copies $4.00 each; 200-499 copies $2.50 each) #585m

How to Read a Paragraph
This guide provides theory and activities necessary for deep comprehension. Imminently practical for students. (1-24 copies $6.00 each; 25-199 copies $4.00 each; 200-499 copies $2.50 each) #525m

How to Write a Paragraph
Focuses on the art of substantive writing. How to say something worth saying about something worth saying something about. (1-24 copies $6.00 each; 25-199 copies $4.00 each; 200-499 copies $2.50 each) #535m

Critical Thinking for Children
Designed for K-6 classroom use. Focuses on explaining basic critical thinking principles to young children using cartoon characters. (1-24 copies $5.00 each; 25-199 copies $2.50 each; 200-499 copies $1.75 each) #540m

For Faculty

Active and Cooperative Learning
Provides 27 simple ideas for the improvement of instruction. It lays the foundation for the ideas found in the mini-guide How to Improve Student Learning. (1-24 copies $3.00 each; 25-199 copies $1.50 each; 200-499 copies $1.25 each) #550m

How to Improve Student Learning
Provides 30 practical ideas for the improvement of instruction based on critical thinking concepts and tools. It cultivates student learning encouraged in the How to Study and Learn mini-guide. (1-24 copies $6.00 each; 25-199 copies $4.00 each; 200-499 copies $2.50 each) #560m